Aspects...

Come affected are tyrants moods.

Nature creates life and food.

Rise to counter all such sins.

Just commit a sin is evil means.

Done and dust are wills of steels.

All are lofty ways as sealed.

Hitch your poses and lift your ways.

TAILISM men are fawn to say.

Men in know is tyrants pets.

States with fairs are good to let.

Partial honest link no parts.

Coming aspects are global marks.

Seven unions are color large.

Fighting laagers all are cars.

Carrier tops are combat jets.

Clear and sweep...

Clear ad sweep are equal laws.

Arms at homes are weapons stores.

Despot stuffs are arms are fires.

Puppet people uses by wires.

Miff and hatred all is ails.

Peoples rights are breath are airs.

China tyrants are damn as stocks.

Damn by gods are some so ought.

Textual books are books that cook.

Burn our jades are ashes to look.

Check ad certain all are bloods.

Tyrants skulls are fruits are nuts.

--------Cheung Shun Sang=Cauchy3-------.

Ease..

Take it ease and let it ease.

Clear but set is army lists.

Lackey eases are kowtow ease.

Easily shocks are humble sense.

Liable simple is simple life.

Heads are hot are peoples lines.

You can fool as laws might hold.

Spam or not is yes and no.

Rare and radiant charms may show.

Taiwan faces are aces to know.

Some are aspects all that trend.

Shysters' laws are ways that bend.

Some are aspects all are norms.

Sorrow looks are bad in forms.

Family labels have grades or scorns.

Essay noon and tyrants..

Colors large are life is noon then very charm.

Seasons come as falls are sad. Sheer to facts are witness words for square deals.

Who buy you as they may win?

Purchase victory with dearly costs or speak the truth with dying courses are tyrants or peoples.

Rising beats are tyrants battle pitches. Inner depth is tyrants PRIAPISM are their stiff laws and orders that is PRIAPISM like. Inner depth of tyrants' minds is self to seek. To be cool down or to be stiff as PRIAPISM is madness of sadness or excites wars. Self assert and self to seek as handle all are tyrants add it all.

Contoured by lines are tools are tasks. All recourses are names of gods. Master tasks are forces that high as sun in noon. Talents hands are tyrants' forces.

Haggard wills are forces that are down but lay and fall. Tyrants the get the dominated courses and better forwards and backwards stands.

Essay-tricks and treats..

Bend your views and ideas to what you may benefit.

Not cases are I.C.A.C.(anti corruption department) cases.

Who benefit our worlds of human with endless treats

and endless efforts?

Gains and losses are conflicted worlds involved lots of

life bargains.

Egoism goes for private-ism always benefit and neglect

laws and mores.

Always benefit self onto large or small profits but

expense other with harms.

Merits and demerit all are goes by re4ckless greed. Tiger

teeth are used by tiger.

Wealth and poses are settled better by tricks and lure by

treats. Laws revised our rules and rules are tricks of

laws.

Marvel all for your progress life as to govern our worlds

or get a very good jobs hence jump for joys of your life.

Make us of laws are rules of leaders usages as leaders or

Essay-all are quarks...

Vulnerable firmness all are tyrants' minds. Beg no to voices that strikes are reviewed comments. Hold and fast are china pure then commie rules. Hold no principal but powers seeking or hyper plugs demagogue massive psychologies.

Solid and compacted are peoples need human right and justices.

Rigid just are peoples' views. Thinks are nouns and acts are verbs. Deeds are phrases and sentences or whole life is manuscripts.

China tyrants iron wills will run amok and kill. Now steadfast all we needed are human ways. Tyrants need forces and powers. They keep them up as esteems or self asserts as clings as leech.

Leeward ways must save us for reddish storms. Who did help us as leeward ways?. Leeward must have forces to come and go and to stop or halt.

Also there should have freedom of speeches or live

Essay-(atone to crimes)...

China tyrants throw their weights about for rounds.

Psyched stir up are stimulus self to missions.

Psyche stir up are united seven. Defy orders against making faults.

Uncle Sam resists tyrants with moral codes at fist but resorted to wars at last.

Oppose china tyranny such would like to combat a flood.

Uncle Sam makes his stand against china over lords.

Fair to play is evenly matches to take china as peoples ways.

Counter china arguments need to have been Uncle Sam.

Convert our life into amounts are money ranks. Feel at spoons are china jesters bribe. Those convinced by china are evil ways,

Most afflict are tyrants who keep us down.

Please atone your crimes and fit at laws.

Do that over and do with pains.

Wrong is DALA lama who said that even pain but not as

Essay-(mood)...

Yogic flying never done as says.

Tyrants' ages are cunning ways.

Yogic flying all are fake.

Sages retreat and fear to stand. Tyrants psycho come and mixed are moods. Tyrants' flies as killing comforted as moods. Tyrants' forces and arms are moods.

So unable nice men will stand and walk as lames.

Stand our grounds and put our words. Gagged rules are raw in laws. Speak our prepared charter bills.

Who can stand so firm without luck?

Keep your feet is Taiwan feet.

Dare to stand are somewhat fun.

Moon NUTATION drive and pass.

Tyrants NUTATION drive our ages.

Moons and planets have gravity good for use.

China tyrants' gravity throws tyrants weights.

Beams and scale as Marxism judges will good to spans.

WUJANTO or Maoism lie to Marxism.'

Poor or rich are ways..

Psychic forces are fools that mad.

Bibles scripts are fable lies.

Crazy of why may bring something justices. Bossy

manners are polar poses. Rancor feels in heart are other

poles. Brimstone fires are bad to all the called and

choose or if and only if the vicious souls,. Evil called and

struggle wild and rude.

Men remain to survive all had to faces the worlds with

music changes. Ever changed are pass and now and

seeking futures.

Our lost situations as poor may only eat of scraps from

riches.

Rich get a hearts that cold. Ruthless cruel all are mad

and self MEGAMONIA life. Just unjust is need and must

teach. Take a scrappy meal and get a warm drink.

Also if worlds have glories then we jealous more and

deeper as days are ways.

What worthy are not only able men. Some sell and buy

Stock to stocks.....

Whether stock up stocks is best to do as moral means.

Our mains are human, peoples, friends, or family.

Peoples live in plenty or people lives in sadness are our topic.

Quite shame and quite shy to know a case is me.

It is about one Hong Kong citizen who saves and takes medical cares for a large five years old abandoned dog.

At the very sense the dog was abandoned and ill that roaming and crouch and sleep with pain on street.

The very kind and good man toke the dog home and cure it.

Latter on other scene I saw from the T.V. tubes and know some more about pets caring.

The scenes show gave the movies about a very scientific and luxurious dog clinic.

The living stocks caring house used very luxurious cares and treatments to dogs.

Dogs swimming pools! Walking machine in other babe

(Essay)- Stormy winds...

Imperial decrees are strong bills.

Weaves of peoples' claptrap are fetish. Lamb instincts

can be very proud. Proud china P.L.A. havoc cries.

Peerless matches are devil sins.

Warriors brave are martial hearts.

Heavy arms are brave tom take.

Valor plucks are lion hearts.

Brave with causes and good are plan.

Urged our man is uncle- Sam.

Uncle Sam is good and gives his hands.

Strains are china tyrants' laws.

Taiwan does Taiwan tasks and bright as lights.

Lights and salts are so and good.

Protect Taiwan best is so good.

General Marshall gets his next kin.

Give no strict injunctions and all must talk.

Cambers laws are well as tasks to pull the bridles.

Squeeze as vicious laws are china ordinance Twenty

Essay-what a tyrant need...

A tale of a tub to break the end is tyrants' lies. Bricks may make as there is mud.

Sterile with causes will lie and die.

China hyper plugs will wear their crown. Laws that dictates and brains that washed. Reach the nth degree is tyrants' spirits. Sway and controls are swaps their rights with gods. Pay it out is swinger party are gods and lords that is over lords. Dramatic persons are items in karma book. So be careful of your manuscripts of live and live-hood.

China head-beeches need no starter as stimulated with thoughts.

There are often lands forfeit with crimes of wars.

Stimulated days of thoughts are sins of lords as china master tasks.

Forged ahead is Taiwan moves as rites and laws.

Rites of passages push for living up peoples freedoms.

Ought to hasten not as death is tyrant written spell that

Essay-some little words about our worlds..

Risk our worlds condemned something go by laws.

Make me bold will fly off our handles. Charm offend is

acts of obsessions. China dictations are peoples

compulsive obsessions.

One will need purity that comes with self controls.

Lurk and hide are latent phase. Laws and ways of olden

brutal worlds are dinosaurs in brains. Large and huge

sinful ways and mind are large as olden dinosaurs.

Latent forces are very hiding forces. Latent sins are

always sins.

Potential threats are china tyrants' wills. Potential

competitions need a better world. China ways are

obtrusive ways.

See the dust of riders and as far behind.

China matches in arms and weapons with the unite

states. China sciences are lagging phases.

Thus the states mostly can take their gains that like

upper hands.

Facts....

P.L.A. will serve their bosses as mains.

Scenes of bloods will keep in brains.

Best to serve are hearts and guts.

Kill a lot are tyrants cuts.

Cut your poses if you are not.

Not in ways are worst are thoughts.

Outfoxed tyrants kill our men.

Kill and hurt are laws to bend.

Keep and earn is self to end.

Throw about and kill with tanks.

Flying wheels are carrier jets.

Bloods and arms are china facts.

Some elected by faction groups.

Some is banned by groups that rough.

CHAU GEE YOUN is victim one.

Forfeit..

Take the passive cases are bones.

Lazy bones have feeble tones.

Acts as hosts are evil lays.

China miffs are peril cases.

Caused by fates are tyrants rule.

China laws have many uses.

All unduly are karma ways.

Darkness come are china ages.

All unduly china truths might seek.

Forfeit china lands and dig.

Psyched and up is Taiwan mass..

China fools will make an ass.

Blind to worship all is jest.

Treat those obey but hurt the rest.

Altered commie like the church,

Forth..

Hard to deal are martial laws.

WUJANTO laws has kiss is forth.

Forth to fronts are graces and charms.'

Rear to keep will do the harms.

JANIFORM form our leaders' forms.

Faith is all for some that wants.

Chief in high have fingers cross.

Bossy commie acts as boss.

Cyclic times are tyrants' times.

Fates are games too real to fine.

Cabal group is heresy built.

Commie party ways are till.

All towards is nothing mad.

Mega mania all is bad.

Mega china mania teaches.

Hong-Kong sweetie slave!..

Norms to alter most is slave.

Slave Cheng TUNK YEE stays.

CORTIN drugs are bad but tang.

Visceral words are lonely man.

Think aloud is ways and sirens.

Sweetie passed but dots are friends.

She had slave and send him boons.

Slave will love her nature wounds.

China public gets the gifts.

Face his music come that if.

Jinx or mascots changed by ways.

Mushroom soups are picks of days.

Mushroom heads are arts of head.

When alive and nose was lead.

Orange smokes might breath and in.

Hyper Functions..

Social changes are people ask.

Social changes are modes are peoples quiz. Modes and rites of passages all will need more and Uprights. Trials and sues are errors prone are lies are shysters games and gamble ways of the accused.

Some to earn benefit as cash that hot or cash that cold.

Refugees quilts and sheets hide no fear or hard to cover them away to cruel worlds.

Dreams have tosses always have nightmares.

The ruled are ill treated.,

Houses many are pens and residents are stock like Living.

Even our masochism had had enough and pledge to stop and leave.

Life is bringing down and cross by trades. Market and official all are big. However all of them lay under top commie leaders.

Sometimes often may jurisdictions all are big timers or

Laws and how...

Lackey ease is kowtow ease.

Saints have fierce or kind as eyes

Smolder angers are rag are putsch.

Storm at you are better rules.

Over lords will rule and trim.

Real as events all are firm.

Real as events all are show.

China forces are why and how.

Jacks of all to trade are now.

Bonze brasses are cheap with cow.

Threat and cow are tyrant modes.

Holly horrors stand as hold.

---------Cheung Shun Sanng=Cauchy3--------

Laws and times....

Defy ones bosses and come and putsch.

Worth to do is who is who.

Taboo violate just are witches.

Truths at homes are bad to teach.

Break the laws that tyrants rules.

Casual jaws are dogs to use.

All must add up all are poor.

Fight for right and who is who.

Violate just are tyrants bans.

Guilty tools have classes and hands.

Try and true is happened causes.

Social Christ is Christ or horses.

Mobs will break our laws by wills.

Feel awkward some are ills.

States with diagrams all can act.

Leading omens..

Lethal weapons some as tanks.

China thug will kill our friends.

Fierce as tyrants malicious come.

Sins that do and devil hummed.

Gain our upper hands the first.

China strike but fail to nurse.

Forget most but not the self.

Leading omen some may shift.

Tyrants self are end and start.

China policy is schemes and arts.

First prevail are first to strike.

First prevail are cause to fight.

Laws deficit come with wills.

Pressed the gangs are ages are new.

Child may train and pick to kill.

Life to judge...

Good to judge are matters ways.

Break off vows are all our days.

Wall may ruin and jades may burn.

Vices will die and bones are urns.

Keep in lines are happy man.

Bring to rear and there are friends.

Off and on are treats are cures.

Settle ways are laws that used.

Hungry men can eat their rice.

Equal laws are something nice.

Garble laws are out of use.

Judge by self is men with ruse.

,

Tricks and ruses are catchy me.

Gentle breezes are good to see.

Gone beyond recalls are calls.

Lucks..

Ways are same to other each.

Greet you gods are you so rich.

Nabobs' words are office means.

Wish you gods are there are dreams.

Train to act and please your bosses.

Wait on you and dreams are tossed.

Wait for lucks our men have funs.

China bosses amok is runs.

Do CORVEE jobs are sad.

Press our gangs are sadism bad.

Catty cats are china ways.

Eyes of cats are jinx of days.

Comply men are tyrants pets.

Teacher pets are life to get.

Fates are doomed are tyrants lucks.

Mold...

Cranial nerves are sparks is cues.

Things reflex is bad to use.

Taiwan china all must null.

Null and void are worst are mold.

Laws imposed are evil wills.

Drink our worlds and down are drills.

Totems tops are career counts.

Happy base are Taiwan towns.

Better bases are mold to search.

Small potato ways may seize.

Some careerists all are hot.

China tyrants lead their hosts.

Goose steps are straps are marches.

Taiwan saints are Joan of Arch.

Mold and forces will cast the steel.

Pains....

Pains in minds will suffer great.

Even lama jerks in seats.

Beaten black and blue will hurt.

Some dementia comes by urges.

Silly wishes are yogic flies.

Silly wishes are all as lies.

Some as notions all may short.

Rarefied music cold is hot.

Rarefied means are yes and no.

Men have wits and dogs have noses.

Rascal men have souls with spirits.

Buddha might is gods with peaks.

--------Cheung Shun Sang=Cauchy3------

Pay..

Pay out ways are smiles and nice.

Only if and just is wise.

Totems things are contour maps.

Who are boss and what to make?

Give you go-by means and wish.

Real to policy all may kiss.

Take a par with laws are just.

Senses of stocks are kin that use.

Totem things are contour high.

Lands are tamed and hills are lined.

Silver clouds have hues of moon.

Pay out fine has coming boons.

---------Cheung Shun Sang=Cauchy3--------

Peony..

Flowers ought to grow with looks.

Swindles words are books to cook.

Trees of peony beauty called.

Signs of wealth are peony all.

Bonds of prisons die for buds.

Seeds will spread on very mud.

Peony dreams are flowers seeds.

Print my books but heads have heats.

Poems and books will like the buds.

Flowers grows are smiles are must.

Peony flowers graces are charms.

Colors hues are good as found.

Grumble made as flowers drop.

Franking stamps are nothing not.

Smells of flowers touch our nose.

Show your heel..

Show your heels and mad to run.

Flee from homes amok that fun.

Need escaped from tiger mouths.'

Break the vows are heavy mounts.

Flee from mad and get the hunts.

Tyrants go amok to run.

Show you hands and show no heels.

Hyper plugs are all to tell.

Flee and hide our fames and praise.

Quick are wits are good and wise.

Mental weakness comes with fears.

Better drinks our men have teas.

Take by ruses and drink my cups.

Cup of beer have bubble up.

Parts of jobs are cut to parts.

Singer tones...

Forge ahead are progress quick.

Taiwan songs are Taiwan keep.

Keep and earn a life that knows.

Taiwan gets their singer tones.

China singers yodel up.

Fetish china tyrants love.

Laugh or weep are tyrants choose.

Evil army walks are goose.

Formula china governs long.

Real is policy so hot.

Serve no purpose should be dirt.

You and me have words for third.

Ill and sick is tyrants' ages.

China needs a larger gate.

Crash no gates and pay your life.

Taiwan lands...

Money banks have cashes are hard.

Lords of soils have soldiers' arts.

Country hosts are whites or brown.

Flash of lights are men in rows.

Noise in white is out of ways.

Noises in brown are stands of days.

Favor places the lays are lands.

Lands relief can fight with tanks.

Grounds to stand are projected maps.

Bases and grounds are Taiwan facts.

Lands and zones have army ranks.

Grounds to grounds are missiles hands.

Handles good are weapons forces.

Grounds to airs are up and more.

Forms of lands are charts are maps.

Wish….

Strikes the centers make the twists.

Whirls are down and up as wishes.

Make the twists at center points.

Guns are heated are plates that boiled.

Wish your names in Darwin ways.

Wish your forces will fall in days.

Tyrants you are bad to say.

Peace might come as gods will stay.

Some as laws are logic made.

Ways of feel are tyrants mad.

Peace is good but there are wrongs.

Peoples' wills are something strong.

Logic points illicit as make.

Logic horns are worst to take.

Conscience ways are wrong or right.

Worst places...

Illegal building parts are good in cost to set up a family of living spaces. They are illegal basements or platform living rooms.

HONG Kong chief executive officer comes out from a small group of mandated leftist men toke a house of better spaces illegally.

Best decor all are human minds but not illegal builds. Fronts have charms and rear is dirt and lies.

This is what is real politic. Real politic exploit and make fairs and honest men suffer.

Thief to treat the thief is C.Y. to Tom Yee LING. TOM YEE LING was other candidates who quarrel for the same pose of C.Y. C.Y. as pronounce by me may be Leung Chau YIN.

In the polling process C.Y. address in public. Some time C.Y. did criticize TOM for illegal building in TOM housing spaces. Latter people discovered that C.Y. had done the same related faults for his family living just

www.ingramcontent.com/pod-product-compliance
Lightning Source LLC
Chambersburg PA
CBHW071559170526
45166CB00004B/1721